Pocket Pal

Jokes
To Tell

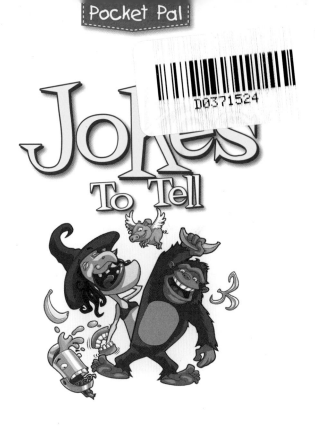

HINKLER
BOOKS

Compiler: Nick Bryant
Illustrator: Glen Singleton
Cover illustrator: Rob Kiely
Project editor: Katie Hewat
Designer: Diana Vlad

Published in 2009 by Hinkler Books Pty Ltd
45–55 Fairchild Street
Heatherton VIC 3202 Australia
www.hinklerbooks.com

10 9 8 7 6 5 4 3 2
14 13 12 11 10

ISBN: 978 1 7418 2120 8

Printed and bound in China

Contents

Animals

What happened when the dog went to the flea circus?

He stole the show.

1

Why are four-legged animals bad dancers?

Because they have two left feet.

What do you call a woodpecker with no beak?

A headbanger.

What do you get when you cross a mountain lion and a parrot?

I don't know, but when it talks, you had better listen!

What do you get when you cross a chicken and a caterpillar?

Drumsticks for everyone!

What do you call a lamb with a machine gun?

Lambo.

What do cats put in soft drinks?

Mice cubes.

What's 150 feet long and jumps every ten seconds?

A dinosaur with the hiccups.

3

What do you call a camel with three humps?

Humphrey.

What do you call a duck with fangs?

Count Quackula.

What did Mr and Mrs Chicken call their baby?

Egg.

What do you get when you cross a rooster with a steer?

A cock and bull story.

Why did the chicken cross the basketball court?

He heard the referee calling fowls.

What do you call an elephant in a telephone box?

Stuck.

Why do elephants live in the jungle?

Because they can't fit inside houses.

What do you call a cow riding a skateboard?

A cow-tastrophe about to happen.

What do you get if you cross a parrot with a shark?

An animal that talks your head off.

Why did the elephant paint the bottom of his feet yellow?

So he could hide upside down in custard.

What's black and white and eats like a horse?

A zebra.

What do get if you cross a centipede with a parrot?

A walkie-talkie.

What did the snail say when he hitched a ride on the turtle's back?

Weeeeeeeeeeeeeeeeeeeeee!!!!

What do you get if you cross a duck with a rooster?

A bird that wakes you up at the quack of dawn!

What do dogs and trees have in common?

Bark.

What's bright orange and sounds like a parrot?

A carrot.

What's tall, hairy, lives in the Himalayas and does 500 sit-ups a day?

The abdominal snowman.

What is a slug?

A snail with a housing problem.

What would you do if a bull charged you?

Pay him cash.

What steps would you take if a bull chased you?

Big ones.

What happened to the dog that swallowed the watch?

He got ticks.

Why is the sky so high?

So birds won't bump their heads.

What time is it when you see a crocodile?

Time to run.

What time is it when an elephant sits on your fence?

Time to get a new fence.

What do you call a baby whale?

A little squirt.

What animal drops from the clouds?

A raindeer.

Why did they cross a homing pigeon with a parrot?

So if it got lost it could ask for directions.

What has four legs and goes 'Boo'?
A cow with a cold.

What do you
call fourteen
rabbits hopping
backwards?
*A receding
hareline.*

Why do gorillas have big nostrils?
Because they have big fingers.

What do you call a fly with no wings?
A walk.

When is it bad luck to see a black cat?

When you're a mouse.

What do leopards say after lunch?

'That sure hit the spots!'

Why did the dog cross the street?

To slobber on the other side.

What's the difference between a barking dog and an umbrella?

You can shut the umbrella up.

What did the duck say to the comedian after the show?

You really quacked me up!

What do you give a pig with a rash?

Oinkment.

Ten cats were on a boat, one jumped off, how many were left?

None, they were all copycats.

What do you get when you cross an elephant with a sparrow?

Broken telephone poles everywhere.

What do frogs order in restaurants?
French flies.

Why does a hummingbird hum?
It doesn't know the words.

How do you know that carrots are good for your eyesight?
Have you ever seen a rabbit wearing glasses?

What does a crab use to call someone?

A shellular phone.

What do you call a sleeping bull?

A bulldozer.

Hickory dickory dock,

Three mice ran up the clock,

The clock struck one,

But the other two got away with minor injuries.

Why do cows wear bells?

Because their horns don't work.

What did the porcupine say to the cactus?

Are you my mother?

MOM... is that you?

What happened to the snake with a cold?

She adder viper nose.

What would you get if you crossed a chicken with a mild-mannered reporter?

Cluck Kent.

What do you call a group of boring, spotted dogs?

101 Dull-matians.

Why can't a leopard hide?
Because he's always spotted.

What did scientists say when they found bones on the moon?
The cow didn't make it!

What kind of dog tells time?

A watch dog.

What do you call a pony with a sore throat?

A little horse.

What do you do with a blue whale?
Try to cheer him up.

Why is a snail stronger than an elephant?
A snail carries its house, and an elephant only carries his trunk.

What is grey with sixteen wheels?

An elephant on roller skates.

What did one firefly say to the other before he left?

Bye! I'm glowing now!

Why was the father centipede so upset?

All his kids needed new shoes.

What do you call a mad flea?

A looney-tic.

What kinds of bees fight?

Rumble Bees.

Why was the bee's hair sticky?

Because he used a honey-comb.

Why did the snail paint an S on its car?

So people would say 'Look at that S car go'!

What do you call two spiders who just got married?

Newlywebs.

How do bees travel?

They take the buzz.

Why did the firefly get bad grades in school?

He wasn't very bright.

What's worse than finding a worm in your apple?

Finding half a worm.

What do you call a fly when it retires?

A flew.

What do you get when you cross an elephant with peanut butter?

Either an elephant that sticks to the roof of your mouth or peanut butter that never forgets.

What do you call a monkey with a banana in each ear?

Anything, he can't hear you.

Now you see it, now you don't, now you see it, now you don't. What is it?

A black cat on a zebra crossing.

Why do tigers eat raw meat?
Because they can't cook.

What do you get if you cross an alligator with a camera?

A snapshot.

What do you get from nervous cows?
Milk shakes.

What's the biggest moth in the world?

A mam-moth.

What's the biggest mouse in the world?

A hippopotamouse.

What's green and wiggly and goes 'hith'?

A snake with a lisp.

Why did the lion spit out the clown?

Because he tasted funny.

What did the beaver say to the tree?

It's been nice gnawing you.

What was the tortoise doing on the freeway?

About three kilometres an hour.

What do you give a sick bird?

Tweetment.

How do you stop an elephant from smelling?

Tie a knot in his trunk.

What should you know if you want to be a lion tamer?

More than the lion.

Why did the fly fly?

Because the spider spied her.

What's the best way to catch a rabbit?

Hide in the bushes and make a noise like lettuce.

What does a porcupine have for lunch?

A hamburger with prickles.

What do get when you cross a dog and a cat?

An animal that chases itself.

What did the goose say when he got cold?

'I have people-bumps!'

What lies down a hundred feet in the air?

A centipede.

What's the difference between a well-dressed man and a tired dog?

The man wears a suit, the dog just pants.

How do goldfish go into business?

They start on a small scale.

How do you spell 'mouse trap' with three letters?

C A T.

How many skunks does it take to stink out a room?

A phew.

If horses wear shoes what do camels wear?

Desert boots.

36

What did the dog say when he sat on the sandpaper?

Rough, rough!

What is more fantastic than a talking dog?

A spelling bee.

What's the same size and shape as an elephant but weighs nothing?

An elephant's shadow.

What did one flea say to the other?

Shall we walk or take the dog?

Where do you find a no-legged dog?
Right where you left it.

How do you get an elephant up an acorn tree?
Sit him on an acorn and wait twenty years.

What did the cat have for breakfast?
Mice Krispies.

Why was the chicken sick?

Because it had people pox.

How do you get down from an elephant?

You don't get down from an elephant, you get down from a duck.

Why do horses only wear shoes?

Because they would look silly with socks on.

What's big, white and furry and found in outback Australia?

A very lost polar bear

Dinosaurs

What do you get if you cross a dinosaur with a vampire?

A blood shortage.

I vant to sark your blurd...

What do dinosaurs put on their French fries?

Tomatosaurus.

What do you get if you give a dinosaur a pogo stick?

Big holes in your driveway.

What do you call a blind dinosaur?

Do-ya-think-he-saw-us?

What do you call a dinosaur that's a noisy sleeper?

Brontosnorus.

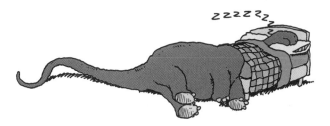

What does a Triceratops sit on?

Its Tricera-bottom.

What do dinosaurs put on their floors?

Rep-tiles.

What do you get when a dinosaur skydives?

A large hole.

What has a spiked tail, plates on its back and sixteen wheels?

A stegosaurus on roller skates.

44

What do you get if you cross a dinosaur with a dog?

A very nervous mailman.

Why didn't the dinosaur cross the road?

Because roads weren't invented.

What do you call a scared tyrannosaurus?

A nervous rex.

What do you call a dinosaur eating a taco?

Tyrannosaurus Mex.

What do you call a dinosaur with magic powers?

Tyrannosaurus Hex.

Miscellaneous

Why is six scared of seven?
Because 7-8-9.

What is scared of wolves and swears?
Little Rude Riding Hood.

What's brown and sounds like a bell?
Dung.

How do you make a hotdog stand?
Steal its chair.

Why was Thomas Edison able to invent the light bulb?
Because he was very bright.

Can a match box?

No but a tin can.

What was more useful than the invention of the first telephone?

The second telephone.

What's small, annoying and really ugly?

I don't know but it comes when I call my sister's name.

How do you use an Egyptian doorbell?

Toot-and-come-in.

How can you tell a dogwood tree?
By its bark.

What invention allows you to see through walls?
A window.

What's another word for tears?
Glumdrops.

Which months have 28 days?
All of them.

When do you put a frog in your sister's bed?

When you can't find a mouse.

Why do toadstools grow so close together?

They don't need mushroom.

What happens when the Queen burps?

She issues a royal pardon.

What did one wall say to the other wall?

I'll meet you at the corner.

Where did the King keep his armies?

Up his sleevies.

Why was the maths book sad?

Because it had too many problems.

What did the stamp say to the envelope?

Stick with me and we will go places.

Where was the Declaration of Independence signed?

At the bottom.

What did the tie say to the hat?

You go on ahead, I'll just hang around.

Why does lightning shock people?

It doesn't know how to conduct itself.

What did the pencil sharpener say to the pencil?

Stop going in circles and get to the point.

What do Alexander the Great and Kermit the Frog have in common?

The same middle name!

What's the easiest way to get on TV?

Sit on it.

What has
four legs and
doesn't walk?

A table.

Where do
you find giant
snails?

At the ends of their fingers.

What's easy to get into but hard to get out of?

Trouble.

Mum, why isn't my nose twelve inches long?

Because then it would be a foot.

How did the rocket lose his job?

He was fired.

What's yellow and wears a mask?
The Lone Banana.

Believe it or not...
behind this mask
I'm really just
an ordinary
banana!

What's brown
and sticky?
A stick.

What do
you call a
lazy toy?
*An inaction
figure.*

Why did the balloon burst?
Because it saw the soda pop.

Why did the bacteria cross the microscope?
To get to the other slide.

What do you do if your nose goes on strike?
Picket.

What's the difference between a TV and a newspaper?

Ever tried swatting a fly with a TV?

How much does it cost for a pirate to get earrings?

A buccaneer.

What is the difference between a jeweller and a jailer?

A jeweller sells watches and a jailer watches cells!

What did the digital clock say to its mother?

Look ma, no hands.

What did Snow White say while she waited for her photos?

Someday my prints will come.

What can jump higher than a house?

Anything, houses can't jump.

Why did the bungy jumper take a holiday?

Because he was at the end of his rope.

Why did E.T. have such big eyes?

Because he saw his phone bill.

What sort of star is dangerous?

A shooting star.

Why did the belt go to jail?

Because it held up a pair of pants.

What is the name of the detective who sings quietly to himself while solving crimes?

Sherlock Hums.

What did the shirt say to the blue jeans?

Meet you on the clothesline – that's where I hang out!

What did the big hand of the clock say to the little hand?

Got a minute?

What kind of music does your father like to sing?

Pop music.

Can February March?
No. But April May.

What's the definition of intense?
That's where campers sleep.

What do you call a man who stands around and makes faces all day?
A clockmaker.

Did you hear the one about the man that went into the cloning shop?

When he came out he was beside himself.

What did one toilet say to the other toilet?

You look a bit flushed.

Why was the archaeologist upset?

His job was in ruins.

Where does a sick ship go?

To the dock.

Did I tell you the joke about the high wall?

I'd better not, you might not get over it.

What did the first mind reader say to the second mind reader?

You're all right, how am I?

What did one ear say to the other ear?

Between you and me, we need a haircut.

Did you know that Davey Crockett had three ears?

A right ear, a left ear and a wild frontier.

What would you call Superman if he lost all his powers?

Man.

What has a hundred legs but can't walk?

Fifty pairs of pants.

I have five noses, seven ears and four mouths. What am I?

Very ugly.

Monsters

What's green, sits in the corner and cries?

The Incredible Sulk.

What do vampires cross the sea in?

Blood vessels.

What did the alien say to the gas pump?

Take your finger out of your ear when I'm talking to you.

Why did the zombie decide to stay in his coffin?

He felt rotten.

What do sea monsters eat for lunch?

Potato ships.

Why did the cyclops give up teaching?

Because he only had one pupil.

Why do witches fly on broomsticks?
Because it's better than walking.

Why did Dracula take some medicine?
To stop his coffin.

What do devils drink?
Demonade.

What don't zombies wear on boat trips?
Life jackets.

What do you call a sleeping monster who won't keep quiet?
Frankensnore.

How does a monster count to thirteen?
On his fingers.

What kind of cheese do monsters eat?
Monsterella!

What do you get when you cross a
vampire and a snowman?
Frostbite.

What do you call a monster that was locked in the freezer overnight?

A cool ghoul.

What do you call a single vampire?

A bat-chelor.

What did the witch say to the vampire?

Get a life.

What do you get when you cross a skunk with Frankenstein?

Stinkenstein.

How can you tell a Martian would be a good gardener?

They all have green thumbs.

What does a monster say when introduced?

Pleased to eat you.

oh hello

78

What do you think the tiniest vampire gets up to at night?

Your ankles.

Why do ghosts go to parties?

To have a wail of a time.

Why aren't vampires welcome in blood banks?

Because they only make withdrawals.

Why do ghosts hate rain?
It dampens their spirits.

What did one ghost say to the other?
Don't spook until you're spooken to.

What do you call a witch that lives at the beach?

A sand witch.

How do you make a witch scratch?

Take away the W.

Why do mummies have trouble keeping friends?

They're too wrapped up in themselves.

How many witches does it take to change a light bulb?

Just one, but she changes it into a toad.

Who is the best dancer at a monster party?

The Boogie Man!

What is a spook's favourite ride?
A roller-ghoster.

What is Dracula's favourite fruit?
Necktarines.

What is a ghost's favourite bedtime story?

Little Boo Peep.

What kind of mistake does a ghost make?

A boo-boo.

What is a ghost's favourite type of fruit?

Boo-berry.

What did the vampire say when he had bitten someone?

It's been nice gnawing you.

What did the skeleton say to the twin witches?

Which witch is which?

Why is the vampire so unpopular?

Because he is a pain in the neck.

What does a ghost do when he gets in a car?

Puts his sheet belt on.

What do you call five witches on a broom?

A car pool.

86

Who did the monster take to the Halloween dance?

His ghoul friend.

What is a mummy's favourite kind of music?

Rap.

Why are ghosts such terrible liars?

Because you can see right through them.

What do you call a dumb skeleton?

A numbskull.

What do you call a vampire's dog?

A Blood Hound!

How do you know when a ghost is sad?

He says Boooooooooo Hoooooooooo!

Did you hear about the ghost who ate all the Christmas decorations?

He got tinselitis.

What do little ghosts play with?

Deady bears.

What is Dracula's favourite ice cream flavour?

Vein-illa.

Why did the little vampires stay up all night?

They were studying for a blood test.

Why did the troll tell jokes to the mirror?

He wanted to see it crack up.

Why do skeletons play the piano in church?

Because they don't have any organs.

How can you tell if a vampire has a cold?

He starts coffin.

What is a witch's favourite class in school?

Spelling.

What does a ghost read every day?

His horrorscope.

Great... it's going to be a terrible day today!

BAD NEWS

Where does Frankenstein's wife have her hair done?

At an ugly parlour.

How does an alien congratulate someone?

He gives him a high six.

How do monsters like their eggs?

Terrifried.

Why couldn't the skeleton go to the dance?

He had no body to go with.

What does a monster eat after he's been to the dentist?

The dentist.

What do you call the winner of a monster beauty contest?

Ugly.

How do you make a skeleton laugh?

Tickle his funnybone.

What do ghosts eat for dinner?

Spook-etti.

Do zombies have trouble getting dates?

No, they can usually dig someone up.

What does a boy monster do when a girl monster rolls her eyes at him?

He rolls them back to her.

Doctor, Doctor

Doctor, Doctor, I have a hoarse throat.

The resemblance doesn't end there.

Doctor, Doctor, what is the best way to avoid biting insects?

Don't bite any.

Doctor, Doctor, I feel like a tennis racket.

You must be too highly strung.

Doctor, Doctor, I feel like a pair of socks.

Well I'll be darned.

Doctor, Doctor, I think I'm a DVD.

I thought I'd seen you before.

Doctor, Doctor, people keep disagreeing with me.

No they don't.

Doctor, Doctor, I'm so ugly what can I do about it?

Hire yourself out for Halloween parties.

Doctor, Doctor, I feel like a dog.

Then go see a vet.

Why do doctors wear masks?

Because if they make a mistake the person won't know who did it.

Doctor, Doctor, I keep thinking I'm a doorknob.

Now don't fly off the handle.

Doctor, Doctor, I keep thinking I'm a dog.

How long has this been going on?

Ever since I was a pup.

PUPPY PHOTOS?

Doctor, Doctor, everyone hates me.
Don't be silly, not everyone has met you yet.

Doctor, Doctor, can you give me anything for excessive wind?
Sure, here's a kite.

Doctor, Doctor, I swallowed a roll of film.
Don't worry, nothing will develop.

Doctor, Doctor, nobody ever listens to me.
Next!

Doctor Doctor, I'm turning into a trash can.

Don't talk such rubbish.

Doctor Doctor, I feel like an apple.

Well don't worry, I won't bite.

Doctor Doctor, I feel like a bell.

Well take these and if they don't work, give me a ring.

Doctor, Doctor, my eyesight is getting worse.

You're absolutely right, this is a post office.

Doctor, Doctor, the first thirty minutes I'm up every morning I feel dizzy, what should I do?

Get up half an hour later.

Doctor, Doctor, I feel like a set of curtains.

Well pull yourself together.

Doctor, Doctor, it hurts when I do this!

Well don't do that.

Doctor, Doctor, I have a ringing in my ears.

Well answer it.

Doctor, Doctor, my leg hurts, what can I do?

Limp.

Doctor, Doctor, I snore so loudly I wake myself.

Try sleeping in another room.

Doctor, Doctor, I have a pain in the eye every time I drink hot chocolate.

Take the spoon out of your mug before you drink.

What do you call a surgeon with eight arms?

A doctopus.

Doctor, Doctor, can you help me out?
Certainly – which way did you come in?

Doctor, Doctor, I'm invisible.
I'm sorry, sir, I can't see you right now.

Doctor, Doctor, I think I'm getting shorter.
You'll just have to be a little patient.

Doctor, Doctor, my sister thinks she's a squirrel.

Sounds like a nutcase to me.

Doctor, Doctor, I keep thinking I'm a dog.

Well get up on this couch and I'll examine you.

I can't, I'm not allowed on the furniture.

Doctor, Doctor, I feel like a window.

Where's the pane?

Doctor, Doctor, I keep thinking I'm a fruitcake.

What's got into you?

Flour, raisins and cherries.

$\mathbf{D}$octor, Doctor, can I have a second opinion?

Of course, come back tomorrow.

Doctor, Doctor, what's good for biting fingernails?

Very sharp teeth.

Doctor, Doctor, what can I do? Everyone thinks I'm a liar.

I find that very hard to believe.

Food

Waiter, you've got your thumb on my steak!

Well I didn't want to drop it again.

Why don't eggs tell jokes?

They'd crack each other up.

What did the banana sitting in the sun say to the other banana sitting in the sun?

I don't know about you but I'm starting to peel.

Waiter, there's a fly in my soup!

Don't worry sir, the spider in your salad will get it!

What is a cannibal's favourite soup?
One with a lot of body.

Waiter, what is this fly doing in my soup?

Freestyle I believe.

What has bread on both sides and is afraid of everything?

A chicken sandwich.

What nut is like a sneeze?

A cashew.

Waiter, I'm in a hurry, will my pizza be long?

No, it will be round.

Waiter, do you serve crabs in this restaurant?

Yes sir, we serve anyone.

Waiter, this apple pie is squashed.

Well you told me to step on it because you were in a hurry.

Waiter there is a small insect in my soup.

Sorry sir, I'll get you a bigger one.

Waiter, there's a bug in my soup.

Be quiet sir or everyone will want one.

Why did the baby cookie cry?

Because his mother was a wafer so long.

Waiter, do you have frogs legs?

No, I've always walked like this.

What did the teddy bear say when he was offered dessert?

No thanks, I'm stuffed.

Have you heard the joke about the butter?

I better not tell you, you might spread it.

What do you make from baked beans
and onions?

Tear gas.

Waiter, how long will my sausages be?

Oh about eight centimetres.

What is red and goes up and down?

A tomato in an elevator.

Why are cooks mean?

Because they beat the eggs and whip the cream.

Waiter, bring me something to eat and make it snappy.

How about an alligator sandwich, sir?

Why did the raisin go out with the prune?

Because he couldn't find a date.

If I had six grapefruit in one hand and seven in the other, what would I have?

Very big hands.

How do you make a sausage roll?

Push it down a hill.

What did the cannibal have for breakfast?

Baked beings.

What did the baby corn say to the mother corn?

Where's pop corn?

What did one plate say to the other plate?

'Lunch is on me!'

Why did the baker stop making doughnuts?

Because he was sick of the whole business.

Gross

How do you make a hankie dance?
Put some boogie into it.

What is the soft stuff between sharks' teeth?
Slow swimmers.

Why are basketball players never asked for dinner?
Because they're always dribbling.

What's green, sticky and smells like eucalyptus?

Koala vomit.

What do you find up a clean nose?

Fingerprints.

What's the last thing that goes through a bug's mind when he hits a car windscreen?

His rear end.

How can you tell when a moth farts?

He flies straight for a second.

What's yellow and smells of bananas?

Monkey vomit.

Just Silly

How did the doofus fall on the floor?
He tripped over the cordless phone!

Why did the doofus climb the glass wall?

To see what was on the other side.

Why did the doofus get fired from the banana factory?

He threw out all the bent ones.

How many fools does it take to screw in a light bulb?

Three . . . one to hold the bulb, and two to turn the chair.

How do you confuse a doofus?

Put him in a round room and tell him to sit in the corner.

How do you get a one-armed doofus out of a tree?

Wave to him.

How can you tell when a doofus has been using the computer?

There is whiteout all over the screen.

How do you keep a doofus in suspense?

I'll tell you tomorrow.

How did the doofus break his arm while raking leaves?

He fell out of the tree.

Why did the doofus get fired from the M&M factory?

Because he threw away all the Ws.

Why did the doofus sleep under his car?

So he would wake up oily in the morning.

How do you sink a submarine full of fools?

Knock on the door.

What happened to the foolish tap dancer?

She fell in the sink.

Did you hear about the doofus who did bird impressions?

He ate worms.

Why did the doofus leap out the window?

To try his new jump suit.

I was just saying a parachute would just finish off that outfit nicely

Why did the fool put a chicken in a hot bath?

So she would lay hard-boiled eggs.

What happened to the stupid jellyfish?

It set.

What did the doofus call his pet zebra?

Spot.

Did you hear about the doofus who got a boomerang for his birthday?

He spent the next two days trying to throw the old one away.

How do you make a doofus laugh on a Sunday?

Tell him a joke on Saturday.

Knock, Knock

Knock, knock.
Who's there?
Alison.
Alison who?
Alison to the radio.

Knock, knock.
Who's there?
Police.
Police who?
Police, let me in.

Knock, knock.

Who's there?

My panther.

My panther who?

My panther falling down.

Knock, knock.

Who's there?

Witches.

Witches who?

Witches the way home?

Come on baby start...!

Knock, knock.
Who's there?
Lettuce.
Lettuce who?
Lett-uce in, it's cold outside.

Knock, knock.
Who's there?
Tank.
Tank who?
You're welcome.

Knock, knock.
Who's there?
Sawyer.
Sawyer who?
Sawyer lights on thought I'd drop by.

Knock, knock.
Who's there?
Freeze.
Freeze who?
Freeze a jolly good fellow.

Knock, knock.

Who's there?

Robin.

Robin who?

Robin you! So hand over your cash.

Knock, knock.
Who's there?
Nanna.
Nanna who?
Nanna your business.

Knock, knock.
Who's there?
Luke.
Luke who?
Luke through the peephole and you'll
see.

Knock, knock.
Who's there?
Boo.
Boo who?
What are you crying about?

Knock, knock.
Who's there?
Justin.
Justin who?
Justin time for lunch.

Knock, knock.
Who's there?
Nobel.
Nobel who?
No bell so I just knocked.

Knock, knock.

Who's there?

Troy.

Troy who?

Troy as I may, I can't reach the bell.

Knock, knock.

Who's there?

Iran.

Iran who?

Iran 25 laps around the track and boy, am I tired!

147

Knock, knock.

Who's there?

Shelby.

Shelby who?

Shelby comin' round the mountain
when she comes!

Knock, knock.

Who's there?

Midas.

Midas who?

Midas well let me in.

Knock, knock.
Who's there?
Miniature.
Miniature who?
Miniature let
me in, I'll tell
you.

Knock, knock.
Who's there?
Arch.
Arch who?
Bless you.

149

Knock, knock.
Who's there?
Little old lady.
Little old lady who?
I didn't know you could yodel!

YODEL-A-EE-OOD

Knock, knock.
Who's there?
Letter.
Letter who?
Letter in or she'll knock down the door.

Knock, knock.
Who's there?
Arncha.
Arncha who?
Arncha going to let me in? It's freezing
out here!

Knock, knock.

Who's there?

Ammonia.

Ammonia who?

Ammonia little girl who can't reach the door bell.

I thought you were a little bug..

Knock, knock.
Who's there?
The Sultan.
The Sultan who?
The Sultan Pepper.

Knock, knock.
Who's there?
Wooden shoe.
Wooden shoe who?
Wooden shoe like to know.

Knock, knock.
Who's there?
Who.
Who who?
What are you – an owl?

Knock, knock.

Who's there?

Despair.

Despair who?

Despair tyre is flat.

I just feel SO DOWN!

Knock, knock.

Who's there?

Weed.

Weed who?

Weed better mow the lawn before it gets too long.

Knock, knock.
Who's there?
Butcher.
Butcher who?
Butcher little arms around me!

Knock, knock.

Who's there?

Winner.

Winner who?

Winner you gonna get this door fixed?

Knock, knock.

Who's there?

Alex.

Alex who?

Alexplain later, just let me in.

Knock, knock.
Who's there?
Radio.
Radio who?
Radio not, here I come!

Knock, knock.

Who's there?

Zombies.

Zombies who?

Zombies make honey, zombies just buzz around.

Knock, knock.

Who's there?

Adore.

Adore who?

Adore is between us, open up.

Knock, knock.

Who's there?

Felix.

Felix who?

Felix my ice cream, I'll lick his.

Knock, knock.
Who's there?
Abbott.
Abbott who?
Abbott time you opened this door.

Knock, knock.
Who's there?
Satin.
Satin who?
Who satin my chair?

Knock, knock.
Who's there?
Celia.
Celia who?
Celia later alligator.

162

Knock, knock.

Who's there?

Irish.

Irish who?

Irish I knew some more knock, knock jokes.

Riddles

What are two things you cannot have for breakfast?

Lunch and dinner.

What has eyes that cannot see, a tongue that cannot taste and a soul that cannot die?

A shoe.

What can you hear but not see and only speaks when it is spoken to?

An echo.

What is there more of the less you see?

Darkness.

What ten-letter word starts with gas?

Automobile.

How many apples can you put in an empty box?

One. After that it's not empty anymore.

When will water stop flowing downhill?

When it reaches the bottom.

What's black when clean and white when dirty?

A blackboard.

What kind of dress can never be worn?

Your address.

What weighs more, a kilogram of lead or a kilogram of feathers?

They both weigh the same.

What word is always spelled incorrectly?

Incorrectly.

What has a bottom at the top?

A leg.

What sort of ring is always square?

A boxing ring!

What's the last thing you take off before bed?

Your feet off the floor.

What starts with an 'e', ends with an 'e' and only has one letter in it?

An envelope.

What is always coming but never arrives?

Tomorrow.

What did the piece of wood say to the drill?

You bore me.

What can you serve, but never eat?

A volleyball.

What do you put in a barrel to make it lighter?

A hole.

What stays in the corner and travels all around the world?

A postage stamp.

What's taken before you get it?

Your picture.

Which room has no door, no windows, no floor and no roof?
A mushroom.

What gets wet the more you dry?
A towel.

What breaks when you say it?
Silence.

What gets bigger and bigger as you take more away from it?

A hole.

What bow can't be tied?

A rainbow.

Why are false teeth like stars?
They come out at night.

What goes all around a pasture but never moves?
A fence.

What has teeth but cannot eat?
A comb.

What can you hold without touching?
Your breath.

What question can you never answer yes to?

Are you asleep?

What starts with a 'p', ends with an 'e' and has a million letters in it?

Post Office.

What goes up and does not come down?

Your age.

What was the highest mountain before Mt Everest was discovered?

Mt Everest.

What goes up and down but never moves?

A flight of stairs.

What runs across the floor without legs?

Water.

What has holes and holds water?

A sponge.

What puzzles make you angry?

Crossword puzzles.

What has four fingers and a thumb
but is not a hand?

A glove.

What cup can you never drink out of?

A hiccup.

What kind of coat can you put on only when it's wet?

A coat of paint.

What belongs to you but is used more by other people?

Your name.

When things go wrong, what can you always count on?

Your fingers.

What flies around all day but never goes anywhere?

A flag.

Where were potatoes first found?

In the ground.

What can you give away but also keep?

A cold.

What has two hands, no fingers, stands still and runs?

A clock.

What is the beginning of eternity, the end of time, the beginning of every ending?

The letter 'e'.

What can't walk, but can run?

A river.

Sport

Why did the golfer wear two pairs of pants?

In case he got a hole in one.

What has 22 legs and two wings but can't fly?

A soccer team.

Where do old bowling balls end up?

In the gutter.

What illness do martial artists get?

Kung Flu.

What position did the pile of wood play on the football team?

De-fence.

When is a baby like a basketball player?

When he dribbles.

Why did the runner wear rippled sole shoes?

To give the ants a fifty-fifty chance.

What's a ghost's favourite position in soccer?

Ghoul-keeper.

What happens when baseball players get old?

They go batty.

What do you get when you cross a football player with a gorilla?

I don't know but nobody tries to stop it from scoring.

Why do soccer players have so much

trouble eating?

They think they can't use their hands.

Why are basketball players always so cool?

Because of all the fans.

Why was the chickens' soccer match a bad idea?

Because there were too many fowls.

Why is Cinderella so bad at sport?

Because she has a pumpkin for a coach and she runs away from the ball.

Computers

Why was the computer so tired when it got home?

Because it had a hard drive.

Why did the computer cross the road?

Because it was programmed by the chicken.

How many programmers does it take to screw in a light bulb?

None, it's a hardware problem.

What Do You Call...?

. . . a man who likes to work out?

Jim.

. . . a girl with a tennis racket on her head?

Annette.

. . . a woman with one leg?
Eileen.

. . . a man with a car on his head?
Jack.

. . . a man who owes money?
Bill.

. . . a man with a spade?
Doug.

. . . a man without a spade?
Douglas.

. . . a girl with a frog on her head?
Lily.

. . . a man in a pile of leaves?
Russell.

. . . a woman in the distance?
Dot.

. . . a man
with
rabbits
in his
trousers?
Warren.

Silly Book Titles

The Invisible Man by Peter Out.

How to be Taller by Stan Dupp

A Terrible Nightmare by Gladys Over.

Famous Frights by Terry Fied.

Strong Winds by Gail Forse.

Swimming the English Channel by Frances Neer.

Speaking French by Lorna Lang Wedge.

Great Eggspectations by Charles Chickens.

How to be Shorter by Neil Down.

Close Shaves by Ray Zerr.

Rice Growing by Paddy Field.

Horror Stories by R. U. Scared.

Up the Amazon by P. Rhana.

The Unknown Author by Anne Onymous.

The Long Walk to School by Mr. Bus.

Infectious Diseases by Willie Catchit.

Exercise At Home by Ben Dan Stretch.

A Bullfighter's Life by Matt Adore.

Broken Window by Eva Brick.

The Mad Cat by Claud Boddy.

The Poltergeist by Eve L. Spirit.

A Ghost in the Attic by Howie Wales.

Explosives for Beginners by Dinah Might.

Egyptian Mummies by M. Barmer.

Ghosts and Ghouls by Sue Pernatural.

The Omen by B. Warned.

Famous People by Hugh Did-Watt.

Jail Break by Freida Prizner.

Dealing With Bullies by Howard U. Lykett.

A Sting in the Tale by B. Keeper.

Clairvoyance Made Easy by I. C. Spooks.

Across the African Plains by Ann T. Lope.

Quick Snacks by Roland Butter.

Sahara Journey by Rhoda Camel.

The Haunted House by Hugo First.

The Millionaire by Iva Fortune.

The Arctic Ocean by I.C. Waters.

Roof Repairs by Lee King.

Easy Money by Robin Banks.

The Rainforest by Teresa Green.

Writing Great Stories by Paige Turner.

Ultimate Hair Care by Dan Druff.

I know You're Lying by Polly Graff.

Making Electricity by Jenny Rator.

Using Adjectives by Des Criptive.

Crossing Roads Safely by Luke Bothways.

Souls and Spirits by Misty Sizzem.

Television Reception by Anne Tenor.

Vehicles

What happened to the wooden car
with wooden wheels and a wooden
engine?

It wooden go.

This one's a real beauty... made from sustainable forests too!
It's got everything! Solid timber construction
full wood interior... 4 good wheels
and... by the look of it....
TERMITES

What did the traffic light say to the car?

Don't look now, I'm changing.

What flies and wobbles?

A jellycopter.

What do you call an expensive car with a cheap name?

A Poor-sche.

When is a car not a car?

When it turns into a garage.

What's a fjord?
A Norwegian car.

What do you give a sick car?
A fuel injection.

What kind of car did Elvis drive?
A Rock-n-Rolls-Royce.

How can you find a lost train?
Follow its tracks.

Why can't a
bicycle stand
up?

*Because it's
two tired.*

Policeman: Did you know that you were driving at 120 mph?

Driver: Impossible. I've only been in the car for five minutes.

What is black and white and red all over?

A newspaper.

Silly Inventions

A parachute that opens on impact.

A left-handed screwdriver

A one-way escalator

An ejector seat on a helicopter.

Glow-in-the-dark sunglasses.

216

An inflatable anchor.

Fireproof matches.

Double-sided playing cards.

Submarine screen doors.

Waterproof teabags.

A solar-powered night light.

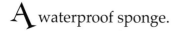A waterproof sponge.

Reusable ice cubes.

See-through toilet paper.

Powdered water.

A dictionary index.

219

A book on how to read.

An inflatable dart board.

Skinless bananas.

Pedal-powered wheelchairs.